DEADLIEST ANIMALS

CROCODILE

BY GOLRIZ GOLKAR

WWW.APEXEDITIONS.COM

Copyright © 2023 by Apex Editions, Mendota Heights, MN 55120. All rights reserved. No part of this book may be reproduced or utilized in any form or by any means without written permission from the publisher.

Apex is distributed by North Star Editions:
sales@northstareditions.com | 888-417-0195

Produced for Apex by Red Line Editorial.

Photographs ©: Shutterstock Images, cover, 1, 4–5, 8–9, 10–11, 12–13, 14–15, 16–17, 18–19, 20–21, 21 (circle), 22–23, 24–25, 26–27; iStockphoto, 6–7, 8 (circle), 29

Library of Congress Control Number: 2022901424

ISBN
978-1-63738-283-7 (hardcover)
978-1-63738-319-3 (paperback)
978-1-63738-390-2 (ebook pdf)
978-1-63738-355-1 (hosted ebook)

Printed in the United States of America
Mankato, MN
082022

NOTE TO PARENTS AND EDUCATORS

Apex books are designed to build literacy skills in striving readers. Exciting, high-interest content attracts and holds readers' attention. The text is carefully leveled to allow students to achieve success quickly. Additional features, such as bolded glossary words for difficult terms, help build comprehension.

TABLE OF CONTENTS

CHAPTER 1
A QUIET HUNTER 4

CHAPTER 2
LIFE IN THE WILD 10

CHAPTER 3
CROCODILE BODIES 16

CHAPTER 4
CROCODILE FEASTS 22

COMPREHENSION QUESTIONS • 28
GLOSSARY • 30
TO LEARN MORE • 31
ABOUT THE AUTHOR • 31
INDEX • 32

CHAPTER 1

A QUIET HUNTER

A saltwater crocodile waits in a wide river. Only its eyes stick above the water. The huge **reptile** is watching for **prey**. Its ears listen for sounds.

A hunting crocodile may float for hours without moving.

The crocodile sees a pig getting a drink. Suddenly, the crocodile leaps from the water. It flashes its giant teeth. Its long tail swishes wildly.

BIG BODY

The saltwater crocodile is the largest reptile on Earth. It can grow to be 20 feet (6 m) long. It can weigh more than 2,000 pounds (907 kg).

Crocodiles swish their strong tails to push their bodies up out of the water.

Crocodiles have the strongest bite of any animal on Earth.

Crocodiles use their sharp teeth to grab and crush prey.

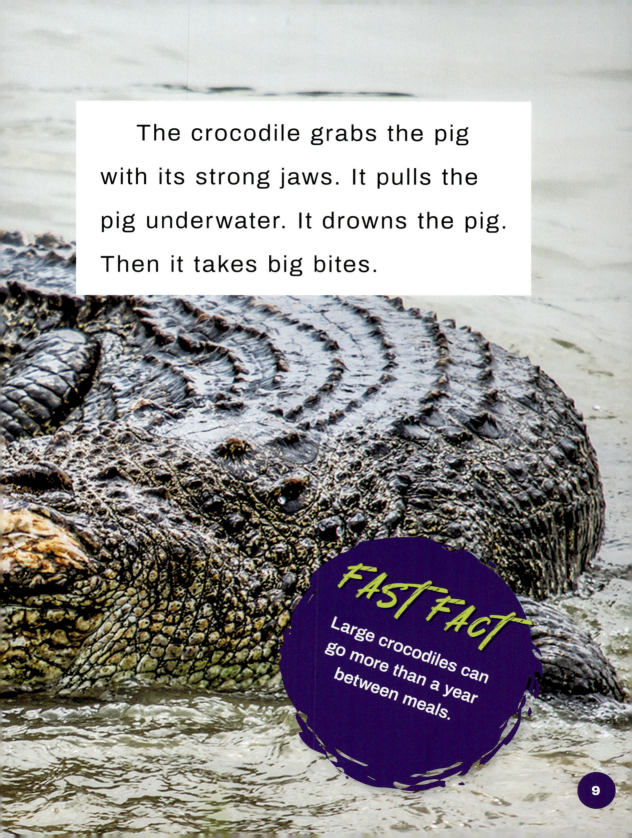

The crocodile grabs the pig with its strong jaws. It pulls the pig underwater. It drowns the pig. Then it takes big bites.

FAST FACT

Large crocodiles can go more than a year between meals.

CHAPTER 2

LIFE IN THE WILD

There are 23 crocodile **species**. They live in **tropical** areas. Saltwater and Nile crocodiles are the most dangerous.

Saltwater crocodiles live in parts of India, Australia, and Southeast Asia.

Some crocodiles swim between fresh and salty coastal waters. Others prefer rivers or **swamps**. Crocodiles move to land to sunbathe or lay eggs.

Nile crocodiles live in rivers and lakes in Africa.

CROCODILE NESTS

Female crocodiles lay eggs. Some bury their eggs in the ground. Others cover them with plants and dirt. These nests keep the eggs warm.

After two to three months, the eggs hatch. Female crocodiles carry their **hatchlings** to water. They watch over their young for about a year.

A female crocodile may have between 10 and 60 babies each year.

FAST FACT

A mother crocodile carries her hatchlings in her mouth. She can hold up to 15 at once.

CHAPTER 3

CROCODILE BODIES

Crocodiles are excellent hunters. They often float near the top of the water. Their bumpy greenish-brown skin helps them blend in with logs and plants.

A crocodile's eyes and ears stay above the water when it hunts.

Crocodiles have short, strong legs. They can move quickly. Some can swim up to 20 miles per hour (32 km/h).

FAST FACT
A crocodile's teeth can grow back if they break or fall out.

A crocodile can hold its breath for an hour or more.

Crocodiles have clear eyelids. They can see underwater. Many crocodiles hunt at night. They see well in the dark.

To stay warm, crocodiles may sleep or sit in the sun.

A crocodile's mouth is full of sharp, cone-shaped teeth.

COLD-BLOODED ANIMALS

Crocodiles are cold-blooded. They sunbathe to warm up. Their bodies take in heat from the sun. To cool down, crocodiles sit in the shade. They may also open their mouths to let out heat.

CHAPTER 4

CROCODILE FEASTS

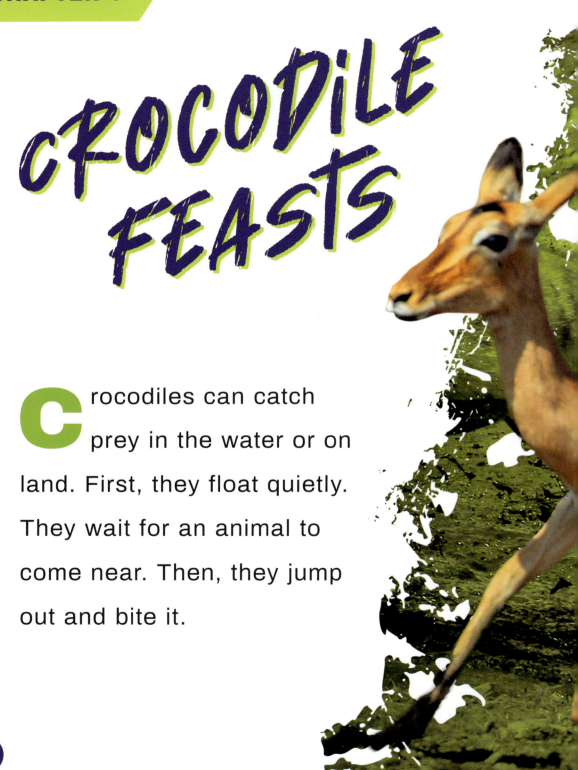

Crocodiles can catch prey in the water or on land. First, they float quietly. They wait for an animal to come near. Then, they jump out and bite it.

Crocodiles can grab animals that come near the shore.

FAST FACT
Crocodiles sometimes throw up bits of food. Then they catch fish that come to eat the bits.

Crocodiles only eat meat. Young crocodiles eat insects, fish, and frogs. Older crocodiles eat birds and small animals. Saltwater and Nile crocodiles may attack large animals.

◀ Some crocodiles attack and eat large animals such as wildebeest.

25

Crocodiles can also be **scavengers**. They eat dead animals in or near the water.

CROCODILE ATTACKS

Crocodiles kill about 1,000 people each year. Crocodiles may attack if humans get near their babies. Sometimes, hungry crocodiles bite people, too. But humans aren't their usual prey.

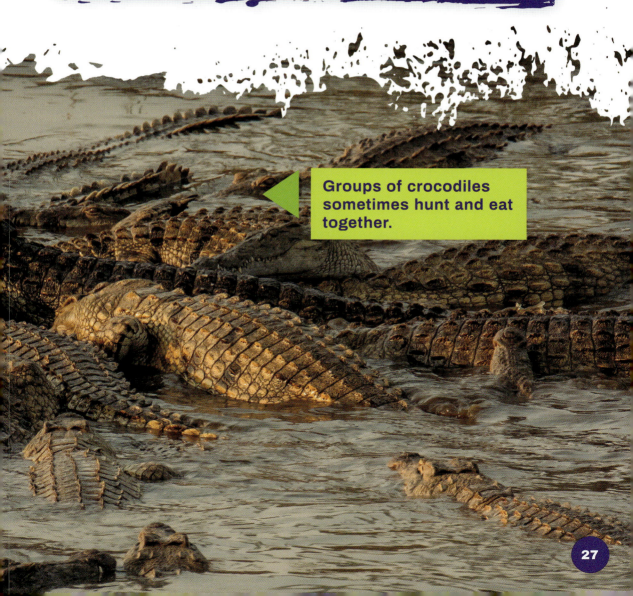

Groups of crocodiles sometimes hunt and eat together.

COMPREHENSION QUESTIONS

Write your answers on a separate piece of paper.

1. Write a few sentences describing how crocodiles hunt their prey.

2. Crocodiles live in tropical areas. Would you rather live somewhere that is hot or cold? Why?

3. What is one thing that crocodiles do to stay warm?
   - **A.** open their mouths
   - **B.** sit in the shade
   - **C.** sit in the sun

4. Why would it be helpful for crocodiles to blend in with plants and logs?
   - **A.** Crocodiles mainly eat plants.
   - **B.** Blending in helps crocodiles surprise and catch prey.
   - **C.** Blending in helps crocodiles swim faster.

5. What does **bury** mean in this book?

Some bury their eggs in the ground. Others cover them with plants and dirt.

    A. to dig a hole and hide something in it
    B. to splash water on something
    C. to guard and keep from harm

6. What does **usual** mean in this book?

Sometimes, hungry crocodiles bite people, too. But humans aren't their usual prey.

    A. most common
    B. possible to see
    C. possible to catch

Answer key on page 32.

GLOSSARY

cold-blooded
Having a body temperature that matches the temperature of the surrounding water or air.

hatchlings
Young animals that have recently hatched from eggs.

prey
Animals that are hunted and eaten by other animals.

reptile
A cold-blooded animal that has scales.

scavengers
Animals that eat dead animals they did not kill.

species
Groups of animals or plants that are similar and can breed with one another.

swamps
Areas of low land covered in water, often with many plants.

tropical
Having weather that is often warm and wet.

TO LEARN MORE

BOOKS
Davey, Owen. *Curious About Crocodiles*. London: Flying Eye Books, 2021.

Murray, Julie. *Saltwater Crocodile*. Minneapolis: Abdo Publishing, 2021.

Simons, Lisa M. Bolt. *Jaguar vs. Crocodile.* North Mankato, MN: Capstone Press, 2022.

ONLINE RESOURCES
Visit **www.apexeditions.com** to find links and resources related to this title.

ABOUT THE AUTHOR
Golriz Golkar is a former elementary school teacher. She has written more than 50 nonfiction books for children. She loves to sing and spend time with her young daughter.

INDEX

B
biting, 9, 22, 27

E
eggs, 12–14
eyelids, 20

F
floating, 16, 22

H
hatchlings, 14–15
hunting, 4–9, 16, 20, 22–25

L
legs, 18

N
nests, 13
Nile crocodile, 10, 25

P
prey, 4–9, 22–25, 27

R
reptile, 4, 7
rivers, 4, 12

S
saltwater crocodile, 4, 7, 10, 25
skin, 16
species, 10
sunbathing, 12, 21
swamps, 12
swimming, 12, 18

T
teeth, 7, 19

ANSWER KEY:
1. Answers will vary; 2. Answers will vary; 3. C; 4. B; 5. A; 6. A